Learn to Draw

DISNEY · PIXAR

ONWARD

Featuring all of your
favorite characters, including
Ian, Barley, Blazey,
and more!

Walter Foster
Jr.

Published by Walter Foster Jr.,
an imprint of The Quarto Group
26391 Crown Valley Parkway, Suite 220
Mission Viejo, CA 92691

Printed in China
1 3 5 7 9 10 8 6 4 2

MIX
Paper from
responsible sources
FSC® C016973
FSC
www.fsc.org

Table of Contents

DISNEY · PIXAR
ONWARD

Long ago, the world was full of wonder. It was adventurous, exciting, and best of all, there was magic...

Now the citizens of New Mushroomton live quiet, comfortable suburban lives with all the modern conveniences, such as gas stations, strip malls, fast food restaurants, and cell phones.

In *Onward*, two teenage elf brothers, Ian and Barley Lightfoot, embark on an extraordinary quest to discover if there is still a little magic left out there.

Tools & Materials

You need to gather only a few simple art supplies before you begin. Start with a drawing pencil and an eraser. Make sure you also have a pencil sharpener. To add color to your drawings, use markers, colored pencils, crayons, watercolors, or acrylic paint. The choice is yours!

drawing pencil

sharpener

eraser

drawing paper

paint palette & paints

colored pencils

paintbrushes

felt-tip markers

How to Use This Book

You can draw any of the characters in this book by following these simple steps.

1.
First draw basic shapes using light lines that will be easy to erase.

2.
Each new step is shown in blue, so you'll always know what to draw next.

3.
Take your time and copy the blue lines, adding detail.

4.
Darken the lines you want to keep and erase the rest.

5.
Add color to your drawing!

Ian Lightfoot

Ian Lightfoot is an elf who lives with his mother Laurel, brother Barley, and pet dragon Blazey, in New Mushroomton. About to turn 16, he struggles with confidence and wishes that his father, who passed away before he was born, was still around to give him guidance.

2

3

4

For the plaid pattern on Ian's shirt, draw a series of crisscrossing lines and use color to fill in the detail.

After setting out on an epic journey with his brother, Ian begins to loosen up and see the world for all its messy, but wonderful possibilities. Perhaps there's more value in the things he already has than he might currently appreciate.

Don't forget Ian's freckles or the slight blush on his cheeks.

Barley Lightfoot

The free-spirited Barley Lightfoot is obsessed with history and fantasy quests. Fun and loud, but a bit naive, this 19-year-old elf may be more into his fantasy world than the real world around him.

Quest Master

5

6

Barley has a lot of patches on his vest. Add as much detail on them as you'd like, or simply color in their basic shapes.

Barley may irritate his brother, Ian, but he will do anything for his friends and family. Selfless and willing to sacrifice for those he cares about, Barley is able to lift up and encourage his brother, Ian, when he's feeling down.

1

8

Barley has a few hairs on his upper lip and chin. Don't forget to add them—but not too many!

Ian & Barley

Barley's understanding of magic and quests are a helpful resource once he and his brother embark on their journey, which tests the limits of Ian's confidence and bravery.

Wilden Lightfoot

Wilden Lightfoot is Barley and Ian's father. He passed away before Ian was born, but he lives on in the form of a magical gift that sends his sons on the adventure of their lives.

1

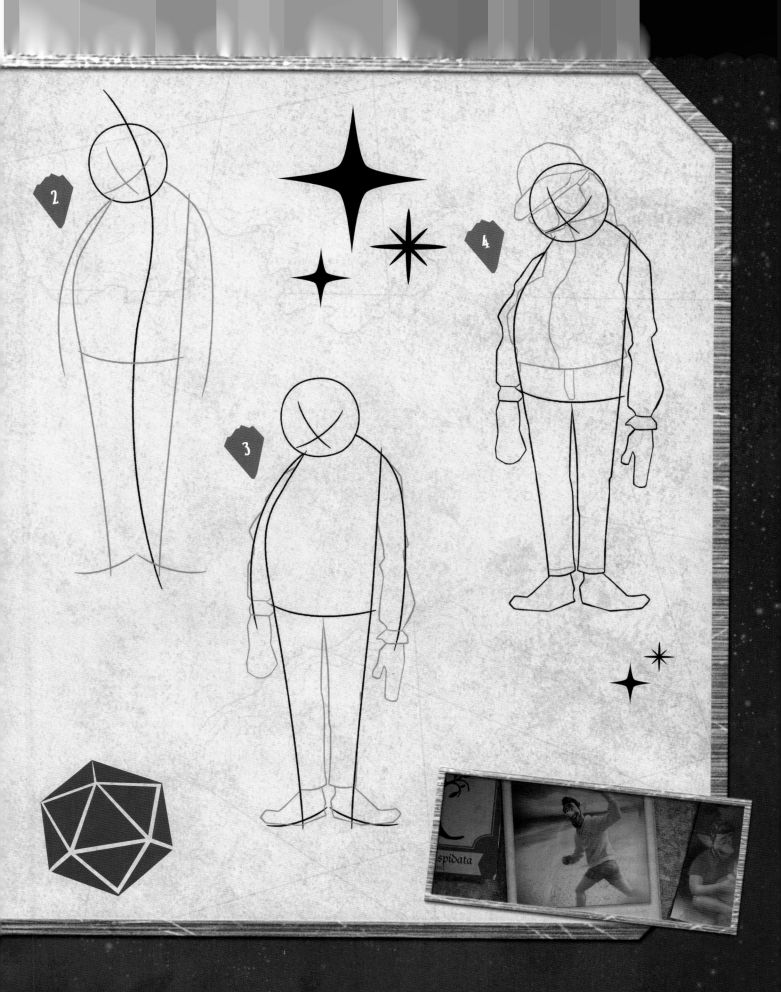

1

8

All these clothes help Wilden
take form, but he didn't
always look this way!

Laurel Lightfoot

Hardworking, quick-witted, and loving, Laurel loves her two boys, Ian and Barley, more than anything. She is determined to keep her promise to raise them well and protect them, no matter how challenging they make that for her.

Color Laurel's sweater
a single cream color and add
some shadows for more detail.
Straight lines down the
front show the pattern.

Manticore

The Manticore—part lion, part bat, part scorpion—was once a mighty warrior, and her tavern was a way station for travelers embarking on epic quests. She is now middle-aged, and her tavern has become a family-friendly restaurant with games, prizes, and fried foods aplenty.

Manticore has lots of curly hair, but you don't need to draw every curl! Add a few lines for detail.

Guinevere

At first look, most would just see a beat-up old van with a pegasus painted on the side, but Barley sees Guinevere as a mighty steed. Built by his own hands, Guinevere may not start right away or have a fully functioning gas gauge, but Barley can guarantee she'll get him wherever his quests lead him.

Don't forget to draw the duct tape and rope holding Guinevere's bumper on!

Colt

Officer Colt Bronco loves his girlfriend, Laurel, and wants to connect with her sons, Ian and Barley, though that is a constant struggle. Colt is strong but clumsy, mainly because he is a centaur (half-horse and half-man). He never seems to notice any of the destruction caused by his graceless back half!

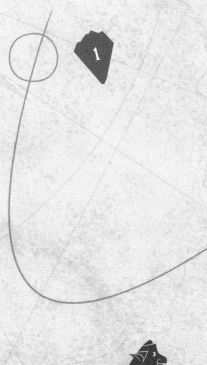

5

6

1

8

Colt has the letters "NM" and "PD" on his collar, standing for New Mushroomton Police Department.

Blazey

Blazey is the Lightfoots' friendly and hyperactive pet dragon. She may be smaller and less ferocious than dragons of old, but Blazey can wreak havoc with just a wag of her tail or a spark of her fire breath.

Each of Blazey's feet has three toes with a sharp nail. She also has sharp teeth and spines down her back.

Dewdrop

As the leader of the motorcycle club the Pixie Dusters, Dewdrop is one fierce sprite. Her most prized possession is her motorcycle, a full-size bike that she drives together with her fellow Pixie Dusters.

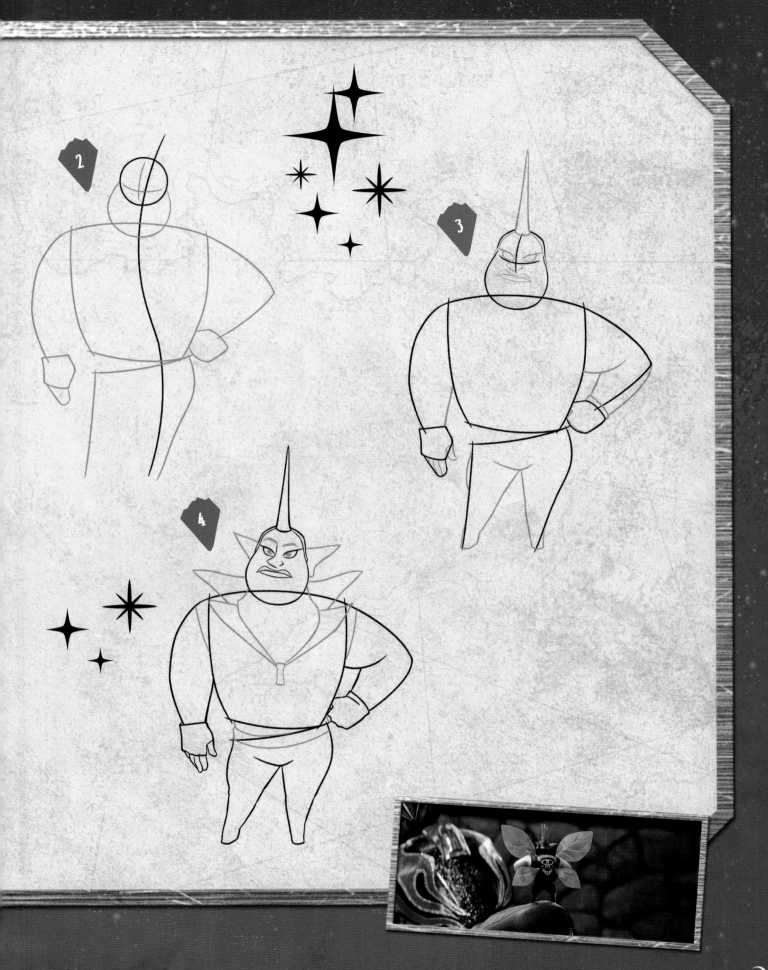

1

8

Although this is a front view of Dewdrop, more than one spike of her pink mohawk are visible.

Specter & Gore

Specter, a cyclops (she has one eye), and Gore, a satyr (half-goat, half-woman), are police officers in New Mushroomton. Specter is a stern, all-business officer who keeps her eye on what's important. Her partner, Officer Gore, is a sloppy know-it-all. She will offer her "expert" opinion whether requested or not.

Unlike Specter or Colt, Gore carries a pan flute in her belt.

Unicorn

The rare, majestic unicorn is a thing of the past. Once a graceful sight to behold, they are now found everywhere, with tattered wings and eating from garbage cans. They are the vermin of New Mushroomton and will hiss at anyone coming too close to their garbage pile.

1

8

To give the unicorn a dopey look, draw one eye looking in a slightly different direction.

Also available from Walter Foster Jr.

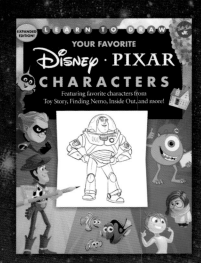

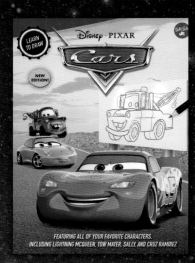

Learn to Draw Your Favorite
Disney•Pixar Characters
978-1-63322-677-7

Learn to Draw
Disney•Pixar Cars
978-1-63322-679-1

Learn to Draw Disney•Pixar
Toy Story Collector's Edition
978-1-63322-763-7

Visit QuartoKnows.com for more Learn to Draw Disney books!